THE SUICIDE CONVERSATION

David W. Carr

First Edition

NEWMAN SPRINGS PUBLISHING
Meadville, PA

First originally published by Newman
Springs Publishing 2025

ISBN 979-8-89617-985-6 (Paperback)
ISBN 979-8-89617-986-3 (Digital)

Printed in the United States of America

To Jayson Holmes, Eric Dunn, The 22,
and all who struggle with suicide.

CHAPTER 1

Shadows in the Mirror

The knock was soft. Three quick taps. Barely enough to register.

Rev. Thomas Benton opened the hospital room door slowly, careful not to let it creak. Inside, the air was stiff with disinfectant and something else—grief, maybe, still hovering in the corners like smoke that hadn't cleared.

The young man in the bed—seventeen, maybe eighteen—had an oxygen tube under his nose, tape across his cheek, IV lines snaking into his arms. His wrists were bandaged. One eye was swollen shut. The other stared past Thomas like he wasn't there.

Thomas didn't speak right away. He just pulled the chair up close and sat. After a while, the boy turned his head slightly, just enough to see him.

"You here to tell me God's mad at me?"

Thomas shook his head. "No. I'm here to tell you He's not going anywhere."

Silence.

That was the beginning of what Thomas called *the suicide conversation*. Not the sermon. Not the lecture. Just the first honest words in a room where death had tried to speak louder than life.

Suicide has always whispered at the edges of human history—unspoken in some eras, shouted down in others, sometimes elevated, sometimes punished, often misunderstood. If you're reading this as a chaplain, a caregiver, or someone walking beside people in the darkest places of their lives, you are stepping into an ancient dialogue. It's not new. It's just been waiting for you.

The ancient lens: honor, shame, and choice

In ancient Greece, suicide wasn't always a tragedy. Sometimes it was a statement. The philosopher Socrates, sentenced to death by the Athenian court, drank hemlock with calm resolve. His students wept around him, but he offered words of peace, of acceptance. He believed in the immortality of the soul. For him, the act was not an escape, but a transition.

The Stoics, like Seneca, believed suicide could be a rational choice—a final assertion of agency when life's virtue had been stripped away. Pain, dishonor, tyranny—these were acceptable reasons. To a Stoic, the moral question wasn't whether someone *died*, but *why*.

Contrast that with the early Hebrews. In the Hebrew Scriptures, suicide is rare and often portrayed with a note of shame or divine silence. King Saul falls on his own sword rather than be captured. Samson brings down a temple on himself and his enemies—a suicide of vengeance. But there is no commendation. No heroism. Just the raw aftermath of broken stories.

In these traditions, life was a gift from God, not to be relinquished lightly. The silence around suicide wasn't indifference—it was a kind of sacred discomfort. A space where even scripture struggled for language.

The Christian turning point

By the early centuries of the Church, something shifted. Saint Augustine—writing in *The City of God*—declared that suicide was a sin, an affront to God's sovereignty. Life belonged to the Creator. To take it was to step into His domain.

This view hardened with time. By the Middle Ages, suicide had become a moral crime. In Europe, those who died by suicide were denied Christian burial. Bodies were buried at crossroads, sometimes with a stake through the heart, and families lost inheritance rights. It wasn't just a personal tragedy—it was a societal violation. The Church wasn't trying to be cruel. It was trying to preserve what it saw as sacred. But in doing so, it silenced countless stories and turned despair into shame.

These centuries still echo in how people think today. Suicide, for many, is still tangled up in judgment—sin, failure, selfishness. As if pain were a crime. As if a dying soul could be saved with scorn. For chaplains, these echoes matter. They're in the room. They're in the questions no one wants to ask. You'll hear them in the way someone says, "He didn't believe in God," or "She just gave up." Beneath the words: *fear*. That death might be final. That pain might mean damnation. You're not there to answer those fears with certainty. You're there to hold them with compassion.

East of here: other worlds, other views

In Japan, *seppuku*—ritual suicide—was once considered a form of honor. A samurai who lost in battle might die by his own hand rather than face capture. It was violent, structured, and public. But it was not shameful.

In India, the ancient tradition of *sati* compelled widows to immolate themselves on their husbands' funeral pyres. Sometimes voluntary, sometimes coerced, it blurred the line between devotion and oppression.

In many Indigenous cultures, suicide was rare but not always condemned. For some tribes, elders who felt they were a burden would walk into the wilderness alone. Not to disappear in shame, but to return to the earth on their own terms.

In Tibetan Buddhism, intention matters. If suicide arises from delusion, it creates suffering. But if it comes from ultimate compassion—such as sacrificing oneself to save others—it may be seen as noble.

These cultural frames aren't relics. They live on in immigrant communities, family traditions, and unspoken expectations. As a caregiver, you are a bridge not just between life and death—but between meanings.

The Enlightenment and the birth of psychology

By the eighteenth century, something fractured. Reason replaced dogma. Faith gave way to inquiry. The Enlightenment didn't solve suicide—it reframed it. Thinkers like David Hume argued that life, once stripped of religious authority, belonged to the individual. Morality wasn't absolute. It was up for debate. The language shifted—from *sin* to *melancholy*, from damnation to illness.

By the nineteenth century, suicide entered the domain of medicine. It became a symptom. Something to diagnose and treat. Freud saw it as the turning of aggression inward. Durkheim, the sociologist, categorized suicide as a taxonomy: *egoistic*, *altruistic*, *anomic*, *fatalistic*.

It was progress, in a way, but it also turned people into problems. As caregivers, we must remember: not all brokenness is pathology. Some of it is soul-deep. Some of it doesn't want fixing—it wants presence.

Suicide in modern times: a shifting vocabulary

Today, we talk about suicide with a mix of clarity and confusion. We use phrases like *mental health crisis* or *completed suicide* instead of *committed*. We try to be sensitive. We try to reduce stigma. But numbers don't lie. Suicide rates are rising—especially among youth, among veterans, among LGBTQ+ individuals, among rural communities, isolated elders, and overwhelmed first responders. Behind each statistic is a story someone didn't know how to tell or didn't feel safe telling, and that's where you come in.

A conversation, not a conclusion

Let's go back to Rev. Thomas and the boy in the hospital bed. The boy didn't say much. Not that day. But he listened. To someone who didn't flinch. Who didn't preach. Who didn't reduce his pain to a mistake. Two weeks later, Thomas saw him again. This time in a coffee shop near the high school. A little less bruised. A little more alive.

"Still think God's not mad?" the boy asked, stirring his drink.

Thomas smiled. "I think He's still listening."

That's the heart of this book. Not to teach you the *right* things to say about suicide. But to help you stay in the conversation. To help you sit in rooms where grief has sucked all the air out. To speak with humility. To listen with sacred patience. To recognize the long shadow of history—and choose to be a light inside it. You are not there to explain why someone tried to die. You are there to walk with them as they decide how they want to live.

Reflection points for caregivers:

- What cultural or religious assumptions about suicide do you carry? How do they shape your instinctive reactions?
- Think about a time when you avoided a hard conversation. What stopped you?
- Consider someone in your care who may be struggling silently. How can you make the unspoken feel safe?

CHAPTER 2

Speaking the Same Language

Before you can help someone out of the darkest corner of their life, you need to understand what they're saying—and what they're not. Words matter. Especially in this work. To enter the suicide conversation with skill and compassion, we must use common language. Not just to label things or to reduce someone's experience to clinical shorthand, but precise language brings clarity—and clarity can save lives. Without shared terms, we talk past each other. We misread pain and miss chances to intervene.

This chapter lays out the essential vocabulary of suicide prevention, not as a textbook, but as a toolkit. These are the terms that shape conversations, guide assessments, and inform decisions. Understanding them is the first step toward being not just a caring presence—but an effective one.

The vocabulary of crisis

Let's begin with the basics. Each of these terms represents a point on a continuum. Confusing them—or using them interchangeably—can have consequences.

- *Suicide*: Death caused by self-inflicted injury with the intent to die. The key word here is *intent*. This isn't an accident. It's not self-harm gone wrong. It's a purposeful act, and recognizing it as such honors the complexity and pain behind the decision.
- *Suicidal ideation (SI):* Thoughts about ending one's life. These thoughts range widely—from vague wishes to escape to detailed plans to end life. SI is often where the conversation begins, and where early intervention can make the biggest difference.
- *Passive SI*: A desire to die without a specific plan or immediate intention. This sounds like, "I wish I wouldn't wake up," or "Life is too much." It's easy to dismiss. Don't. Passive SI is often the mind's quiet SOS signal.
- *Active SI*: Involves thoughts of suicide *with* a method or plan in mind. "I've thought

about using pills." "I've thought about stepping in front of a train." This moves the person closer to action. The risk is higher. So is the urgency.

- *Suicide attempt*: A self-inflicted, potentially harmful act carried out with the intent to die, but that does *not* result in death. It's not a failure. It's a critical moment—one that demands immediate attention, care, and often a reassessment of support systems.
- *Non-suicidal self-injury (NSSI)*: This includes behaviors like cutting, burning, or hitting oneself—not as an attempt to die, but to cope with overwhelming emotion. It can be confusing. The key difference is *intent*. NSSI is not about death. It's about relief, control, or expression, and it's often misunderstood.
- *Suicide cluster*: A group of suicides or attempts that happen close together in time or location. Clusters often affect schools, small towns, or peer groups. They require coordinated public health responses, not just pastoral presence. They can spread like a virus: not through imitation, but through shared despair.

Understanding these terms isn't academic—it's pastoral. Each term helps you name what you're seeing, hearing, and sensing. And names have power.

The role of intent: the heart of the matter

Of all the words in the suicide vocabulary, *intent* is the most critical—and the most slippery.

Intent refers to a person's desire and determination to die by suicide. It is not the same as suicidal thoughts. Someone may *think* about suicide for years and never truly *intend* to act. Others may move from idea to intent in hours, in a moment of crisis.

Intent is what changes everything.

It's how we distinguish between a cry for help and a plan for death. It's how we decide whether to offer comfort, call for backup, or remove access to lethal means. It guides us in real time.

Here's how intent shows up in practice:

Element	Example Question	Significance
Passive ideation	"Do you ever wish you wouldn't wake up?"	Low intent; signals emotional exhaustion or depression

Active ideation	"Have you thought about taking your own life?"	Medium concern; moving closer to risk
Intent to act	"Do you want to die?"/"Do you plan to go through with it?"	High concern; strong predictor of acute risk
Lethality of plan	"Have you decided how or when?"	Very high concern; requires immediate safety action

When someone says, "I want it all to stop," that's *ambivalence*. When someone says, "I've bought a gun, and I'm waiting until Friday," that's *intent with means*. Those are two very different emergencies.

Impulsivity vs. planning

Suicide isn't always planned. Some attempts are made in a flash—after a breakup, a moment of shame, or a public humiliation. This is more common in adolescents and young adults, where emotional regulation is still developing. Other suicides are the opposite: slow, deliberate, written into journals, rehearsed. Both require urgent care. But they're not the same. Impulsive behavior may signal emotional dysregulation, trauma, or access to lethal means. Planned attempts may suggest deep, sustained psychological pain and resignation. In both cases, *intent* helps shape how you respond, and how quickly.

Intent as a guide to intervention

Once you understand a person's intent, your response becomes clearer.

Level of Intent	Recommended Intervention
No suicidal intent	Supportive counseling, regular follow-ups, and addressing underlying distress
Uncertain or ambivalent intent	Motivational interviewing, engaging in deeper exploration, and developing a safety plan
Clear intent with a plan	Immediate intervention: hospitalization, crisis team, remove access to means

The goal is not to panic. It's to match the response to the need. Overreacting to passive ideation can drive people into silence. Underreacting to active intent can cost a life.

Cultural and contextual complexity

Intent doesn't always speak clearly. In some cultures, direct talk about suicide is taboo. In others, metaphors and stories replace confession. A teenager from a conservative religious family may talk in riddles—"I'm tired of pretending," "God wouldn't care if I disappeared." A veteran might downplay their feelings—"It's just noise in my head." And in some cases, people *do* express suicidal language without wanting to die. They want to be heard. To make someone notice. This doesn't mean it's *manipulation*. It means pain has outpaced their coping tools. Always listen for the truth beneath the language. That's where intent lives.

Hope changes intent

Here's the good news: intent is fluid. It's not fixed. It changes with:

- *Connection*—When someone knows they are not alone, their intent to die often weakens.
- *Pain relief*—Not just physical pain, but psychic pain—shame, fear, guilt, despair.
- *Coping strategies*—When people have tools, they are more likely to wait. To breathe. To reach out.

- *Hope and meaning*—When someone believes tomorrow might hold something different, suicide loses its grip.

Your presence can be part of that shift. Not by offering platitudes, but by helping someone imagine a life beyond this moment.

Why it matters

In pastoral care, it's tempting to fall back on comfort phrases. "You matter." "Don't give up." "God has a plan." These aren't wrong, but they're not always enough.

You need to know what kind of pain you're speaking into. You need to recognize where someone is on the map. That's what shared language does. It turns a wilderness into something you can navigate—together. You don't need to be a clinician to use this language. You just need to be committed to accuracy and empathy, to stay with someone long enough to help them find a different kind of story.

Intent is the heartbeat of suicide risk. It gives us a window into a person's readiness, their danger, and their possible road back. But it doesn't live in isolation. It must be understood in context—of culture, history, pain, and relationships.

Reflection points for caregivers:

- Have you ever confused passive suicidal ideation with active intent? What were the consequences?
- How confident are you in assessing intent? What questions do you use?
- Have cultural or personal beliefs ever shaped how you respond to suicidal language?

CHAPTER 3

The Ethics of Being Present

The fluorescent lights buzzed faintly above the crisis intake room, casting a pale hue across the vinyl chairs and worn linoleum. Rev. Lisa Jordan sat across from a middle-aged man in wrinkled hospital scrubs. His hands were clasped; his eyes fixed on the floor. The name on the chart was *Michael T., forty-eight.* Suicide attempt via overdose. Found by his ex-wife. Revived with Narcan. Now awake, lucid, and furious.

"I didn't ask to be saved," he said, his voice tight. "You think dragging me back from the edge fixed anything?"

Lisa didn't answer right away. She'd learned that the best conversations about suicide didn't start with answers. They start with respect.

"I don't think it fixed anything," she said softly. "But I'm here because you're still here. And that matters to me."

He looked at her—actually looked this time.

"Why?" he asked.

That's the real question in this work. Not just *what do we do*—but *why* do we do it? And what right do we have?

That's where ethics begins.

More than a skillset

Suicidology is often approached like a science—and it *is*. Risk factors, data models, psychopharmacology, protective frameworks. These are essential, but when someone is holding a bottle of pills, sitting on the edge of a bridge, or texting their goodbye in the dark—what they need most is not analysis. They need someone who shows up *ethically*. Because ethics is not about abstract philosophy. It's about *how we treat people in their pain*. And in suicidology, ethics is more than a backdrop. It's the ground we stand on.

Ethical practice in suicide prevention rests on five foundational pillars that guide every decision, interaction, and intervention. These pillars—*beneficence*, *non-maleficence*, *autonomy*, *justice*, and *fidelity*—form the moral compass for anyone supporting individuals in crisis. Beneficence calls us to actively promote healing and well-being, while non-maleficence reminds us to avoid causing further harm, even unintentionally. Autonomy challenges us to respect each person's right to make choices, even in distress, while balancing the need for safety. Justice compels us to confront systemic inequities and ensure fair, inclusive access to care. Finally, fidelity is the commitment to integrity, confidentiality, and trust—the very foundation of meaningful, compassionate support. Together, these five pillars offer not just an ethical framework but a path to presence, accountability, and hope in the face of profound human suffering. Here's a closer look.

Beneficence: to help is our first instinct

Beneficence means actively promoting the well-being of others. It's the reason most chaplains and caregivers entered this field in the first place: to be a force for good. But in suicide prevention, *helping* is complicated.

When Lisa sat with Michael, she didn't try to talk him out of anything. She listened. She asked if he wanted water. She found out he had a daughter, that he used to play guitar, and that he'd once spent three years sober before everything unraveled. Her support wasn't flashy. It was deliberate. Beneficence isn't about fixing someone. It's about offering a steady, life-affirming presence in moments where life feels unbearable.

In practice, beneficence looks like:

- Calling in a therapist when you're out of your depth.
- Supporting someone through a safety plan, even if they're not sure they want one.
- Asking, "What would help you feel more in control right now?"

We promote life by being committed to *dignity*, not just survival.

Non-maleficence: first, do no harm

Sometimes, we hurt when we think we're helping. You tell someone they're *being selfish* for thinking about suicide, and they shut down. You call their emergency contact without telling them—and now they feel betrayed. You minimize their pain by saying, "You have so much to live for"—and they feel more alone than ever. Non-maleficence isn't just about *avoiding mistakes*. It's about being *intentionally careful*. Words have consequences. Silence does too.

In suicidology, harm can come from negligence *or* overreach. Consider this:

A well-meaning youth pastor pressures a teen to confess suicidal thoughts in front of the group. The teen smiles, denies everything, and never returns.

What went wrong? A failure to understand emotional safety. A failure to respect privacy. A failure of non-maleficence.

Before you act, ask:

- Will this make them feel more safe or more surveilled?
- Am I acting from their needs—or my fear?
- Could my intervention cause unintended harm?

Being ethical means pausing before you act—and remembering that caution is a form of compassion.

Autonomy: the hardest tension

Few principles are more complicated than *autonomy* in suicidology. If someone wants to die, do we have the right to stop them? If we force hospitalization, are we protecting them—or violating them?

If we withhold information to *keep them safe*, are we preserving life—or undermining trust? There are no easy answers. But the ethical principle is clear: **we must honor personal agency *while also protecting life.*** That means:

- Involving individuals in decisions whenever possible.
- Asking for consent before involving others—unless they're at imminent risk.
- Respecting the choices someone *can* make, even when others are taken off the table for safety.

Michael—sitting in that ER—was still furious hours later. But when the psychiatrist came in, Lisa stayed. She helped translate medical language. She asked Michael if he wanted her there before the interview started. She advocated for his right to speak for himself. That is *ethical advocacy*. Supporting autonomy means offering information, choices, and *respect*—not just containment.

Justice: who gets help?

Here's the hard truth: suicide prevention isn't equally accessible. Black youth are less likely to be referred for mental health treatment, even when they show clear signs of distress. LGBTQ+ teens are more likely to be criminalized than counseled. Indigenous communities face disproportionately high suicide rates—and disproportionately low resources. Justice means more than good intentions. It means action. It means:

- Recognizing who gets overlooked.
- Challenging the systems that make access unequal.
- Making room for cultural context in how we interpret risk.

One chaplain told the story of a Latina woman in her church who had expressed suicidal thoughts after her husband was deported. A white mental health worker dismissed it as *drama*. The chaplain didn't. She listened and validated. She connected her with a bilingual grief counselor. *Justice starts with belief.* When someone tells you they're in pain—believe them, especially if the world often doesn't.

Fidelity: trust is everything

A person with suicidal ideations often has one critical question: *Can I trust you?* Trust is the currency of intervention. You can have every credential, every technique—but if someone doesn't trust you, you have nothing.

Fidelity means:

- Being honest about what you can and can't keep confidential.
- Following through on what you say you'll do.
- Never use vulnerability against someone.

In crisis care, you may need to break confidentiality to protect a life. But *how* you do it matters. You can say:

"You've shared something really serious with me. I want to honor your trust *and* make sure you stay safe. That means I need to bring in some additional support. I'll stay with you through the whole process, if you want me to."

Fidelity isn't just about secrecy. It's about integrity. It's the tone you use. The way you look someone in the eye. The promise that even if things get hard—you won't disappear.

A field of gray

Ethics in suicidology isn't clean. You will face situations where:

- Doing the right thing angers the person you're trying to protect.
- Cultural values clash with clinical expectations.
- You must act without complete information.
- You're afraid of saying or doing the wrong thing, and someone's life is on the line.

That's not failure. That's the terrain of this work. The ethical caregiver doesn't pretend to know everything. They commit to showing up with compassion, courage, and accountability. They ask hard questions. They seek feedback and hold space for complexity.

Epilogue: the exit door

Michael was discharged three days later. Voluntary stay. Safety plan in place. A referral to a peer support group. Lisa called to check in a week later.

"Still here," he said over the phone. "Don't know if I'm glad about that. But…thanks for not treating me like a screwup."

She smiled. "You're not. You're human."

That's what ethics comes down to—seeing the human, protecting the human, respecting the human, even when they don't see it themselves.

Reflection Points for Caregivers

- When have you been unsure whether to protect someone's autonomy or prioritize their safety? How did you decide?
- Have you ever caused harm unintentionally through your words or actions? What did you learn from that?
- What biases might influence whose pain you believe—and whose you dismiss?

- How do you maintain trust with people in crisis, especially when confidentiality must be broken?
- In what ways can you promote justice in your own setting—through language, referrals, access, or advocacy?

CHAPTER 4

The Weight of Words: Stigma, Language, and the Silence That Kills

It was just after the Wednesday night prayer circle when Melissa stopped by Rev. Henry's office. She hovered in the doorway. "I don't know if I should say this," she started. "It's probably stupid."

Henry looked up from his desk. "Come in. You don't have to decide that alone." She sat, eyes down.

"My sister," she said. "You know she died three years ago."

Henry nodded. "In the car accident. I remember."

Melissa's voice cracked. "That's what we told people. It wasn't an accident. She…she took her own life." Silence. The kind that makes your lungs tighten. "We didn't want anyone in church to know. My parents thought it would ruin her memory. I did too, for a while." Henry stayed quiet. Let her fill the space. "But the shame..." she said. "It's worse than the grief. I wish we could've just said it. I wish she could've said something *before* it happened. But I think... I think she didn't because she thought we'd all think she was broken."

How many lives might be saved—not just helped, but *truly saved*—if people felt safe enough to say, "I'm not okay"? Not whispered in the dark or scribbled at the end of a suicide note but spoken out loud, in the light, with the hope that someone would hear and hold it. Let's talk about why that so often doesn't happen. Let's talk about *stigma*—and the language we use that either fuels it or breaks it down.

Understanding stigma: the silent killer

Stigma doesn't just create discomfort. It creates *danger*. It builds invisible walls around pain and turns suffering inward. It isolates. It silences. And silence can kill.

1. Public stigma

Public stigma is the collective judgment of society. It's the tight-lipped expression when suicide is mentioned. It's people changing the subject when they hear, "He died by suicide." It's the whisper: "That family has *issues*."

You've seen it:

- In churches that refuse to acknowledge mental illness as real.
- In workplaces where taking time off for depression is a liability.
- In schools where a suicide is swept under the rug *to protect reputations*.

Public stigma tells people, in a hundred subtle ways: "*You're not safe here. Keep that part of you hidden.*" And when people hide, they suffer alone.

2. Self-stigma

Now imagine absorbing that judgment. Imagine internalizing it. Self-stigma is when the outside message becomes the inside voice.

"What's wrong with me?"

"I shouldn't feel this way."

"If anyone knew, they'd leave."

"I'm not strong enough. I'm not good enough."

Self-stigma isn't just shame—it's shame turned inward until it becomes part of someone's identity.

That's when suicidal ideation becomes more dangerous. Not just because someone is hurting—but because they start to believe they don't deserve help. Language is never neutral. Every word we speak either invites someone out of hiding—or pushes them deeper into it.

▢ *Field Tip:* When someone says, "I shouldn't feel this way," don't argue. Say, "I hear that. But I'm here with you anyway."

Words that harm

Some phrases are so common, we don't notice them. But they sting.

- "Committed suicide"—The word *committed* implies sin or crime. We commit theft. We commit murder. This phrase carries shame, suggesting that suicide is immoral or illegal. For someone grieving or struggling, that word can cut deep.
- "Successful/failed suicide"—Think about that. If someone dies, we call it *successful.* If they survive, we say they *failed.* What kind of message does that send?

These words may be unintentional, but their impact is real. They attach judgment to pain.

■ *Real Story*: A young man named Jordan survived a suicide attempt. A doctor asked, "So you failed?" Jordan later said, "I felt like I didn't belong anywhere—not even as a suicide."

Words that heal

We can do better. We *must* do better. Use language that affirms humanity and dignity:

- "Died by suicide"—A neutral, factual phrase. No judgment. No criminal overtones.
- "Survived a suicide attempt"—This focuses on life, not failure.
- Person-first language—Say: "A person experiencing suicidal thoughts." Not: "A suicidal person." Their identity is not their pain.

□ *Field Tip*: Model this in every interaction. Language isn't just vocabulary—it's culture. And culture is what makes safety possible.

You might wonder: Is it really *just* words? Yes—and no. Because language doesn't exist in isolation. It shapes:

- How we write policies.
- How we craft sermons.
- How a teenager googles their symptoms.
- How a parent tells their child they're struggling.
- How someone describes their own worth.

Language creates *permission*. Or it reinforces *silence*.

■ *Exercise*: Read these two statements:

- "She committed suicide after a failed attempt last year."
- "She died by suicide after surviving an attempt last year."

Which one honors her humanity? Which one opens a door to empathy?

What you can do: changing the culture, one conversation at a time

This work doesn't belong just to clinicians or media professionals. It belongs to *you*—chaplains, caregivers, advocates, parents, friends. Anyone with a voice.

1. Examine your own language

Start with yourself. We all have linguistic habits. Challenge them. Ask:

- Where did I learn this term?
- What does it imply?
- Does it match my values as a caregiver?

2. Gently correct others

When someone says "committed suicide," you don't have to shame them. Try: "I used to say that too. But I learned that *died by suicide* is more respectful and accurate." Correction becomes an invitation when offered with grace.

3. Model compassionate communication

In your workplace, your congregation, your dinner table—talk about suicide like you would any health issue. Calmly. Respectfully. Without fear.

Normalize phrases like:

- "It's okay to not be okay."
- "Let's talk about what you're going through."
- "You can say hard things here."

4. Center lived experience

When we listen to those who have struggled and survived, we learn how our words affect real lives. Their insights must guide us. We can build crisis lines. We can create protocols. We can train professionals. And we should. But none of that matters if people feel too ashamed to speak up.

The way we talk about suicide matters. Because behind every statistic is a person—someone's friend, parent, sibling, child. Someone who might be sitting silently in the room with you, waiting to see if it's safe to say, *"I'm not okay."*

Make it safe. Make it kind. Make it human.

Back in Rev. Henry's office, Melissa wiped her eyes. "You're the first person I've ever told the truth," she said.

Henry nodded. "Thank you for trusting me with it."

She stood, paused. "Do you think…if we'd talked about it back then, if she hadn't felt like she had to hide…do you think she might still be here?"

Henry didn't offer easy answers. "I don't know. But I know this—your voice just made it easier for the next person to speak."

☐ *Reflection Points for Caregivers*

- What phrases about suicide have you used without realizing their impact?
- When have you heard someone speak with shame about their mental health? How did you respond?
- What cultural or religious messages around suicide still influence your language?
- How might you lead a shift in your community's language—gently, consistently, effectively?

📋 Language Shift Quick Guide

Harmful Term	Better Language
Committed suicide	Died by suicide
Failed attempt	Survived a suicide attempt
Suicidal person	A person experiencing suicidal thoughts
Successful suicide	Suicide death
Attention-seeking	Expressing distress

CHAPTER 5

The Sacred Trust and the Necessary Line: Confidentiality and the Duty to Warn

Chaplain Kara Fielding was halfway through her third cup of coffee when Ethan walked into her office. He didn't knock. He didn't need to. He came every Thursday morning after group, usually just to sit. But this morning, he didn't sit. He stood in the doorway, his hands shoved deep into his hoodie pockets, his eyes bloodshot and restless. "I need to say something," he said.

Kara closed her notebook. "Okay."

"It's serious."

She nodded slowly. "Go ahead."

He took a breath. "I think I'm gonna do it. Not today, maybe, but soon. I've been planning. I even picked the spot."

Silence.

A deep, holy silence. The kind where everything else fades and only the truth remains.

The value of confidentiality

Confidentiality is more than policy. It is *a sacred trust*—a covenant between the caregiver and the person seeking help. It tells the struggling soul: You *are safe here. You can speak without fear.* When a person shares their pain with a chaplain, it is often the first time they have named it out loud. That act of vulnerability is terrifying. Confidentiality calms the storm. It builds the bridge for honesty, for rawness, for truth.

Why it matters

- *It builds trust.* Without confidentiality, there is no relationship—only performance.
- *It fosters safety.* A safe space allows the truth to surface.
- *It opens doors.* People who feel safe will talk about their pain—and their risk.

Chaplains often become the keepers of confessions and the protectors of secrets that are too heavy for the world to hold, but what happens when that secret is a plan to die?

The limits of confidentiality: duty to warn and protect

Confidentiality has limits. And when the line is crossed—when someone is in imminent danger—*you are not only permitted but required to act.* This is called the *duty to warn* or *duty to protect.* It exists not to punish, but to preserve life. Let's break this down.

What is the duty to warn/protect?

The duty to protect emerges when someone is at credible risk of serious harm to themselves or others. The professional—chaplain, counselor, clinician—then has a moral, ethical, and often legal obligation to break confidentiality *to prevent harm.* It may mean:

- Notifying law enforcement or a crisis team.
- Contacting a mental health professional or emergency services.
- Warning a potential victim (in rare but clear cases of targeted threat).

Where it comes from: legal roots

The concept has legal precedent:

- *Tarasoff v. Regents of the University of California (1976).* Established that therapists must take action when a client makes a credible threat against a third party. Originally framed as *duty to warn*, this was refined into a broader *duty to protect.*
- *Jablonski by Pahls v. United States (1983).* Extended responsibility to reviewing a patient's treatment history and acting on prior threats—not just current disclosures.
- *Ewing v. Goldstein (2004).* Held that threats communicated through a third party (e.g., a family member) can still trigger the duty to protect.

While these cases focus on third-party threats, the principles are applicable to self-harm. When suicide risk is foreseeable and imminent, the caregiver has a duty to act—even if it means breaking trust.

The balancing act

As chaplains and caregivers, we are always walking a tightrope: Honor *privacy. Protect life.* It's not always clear when to intervene. But this rule can guide you: *Confidentiality is the rule. Safety is the exception.* And when that exception arises, it must be handled with care, humility, and clarity.

How to navigate these situations

1. Assessing risk

You are not a diagnostic machine. But you *can* learn to recognize danger. Look for:

- *Specific plans* ("I've bought the rope," "I picked the bridge").
- *Access to lethal means* (firearms, medications, etc.).
- *Recent changes* (withdrawal, giving away possessions, sudden calm after deep depression).
- *Statements of hopelessness* ("There's no way out," "I can't do this anymore.")

□ *Field Tip:* If someone says, "I've thought about it," ask, "Do you have a plan? Do you intend to act on it?"

When *intent*, *plan*, and *means* align, the risk is high.

2. Steps to take when a risk is imminent

- *Clarify your limits upfront.* "What you share with me is private—unless you talk about hurting yourself, someone else, or if I believe someone is in danger. Then I have to act to keep people safe."
- *Document everything.* Record what was said, your observations, who you contacted, and what actions were taken.
- *Consult.* If unsure, speak with a supervisor, ethics board, or legal counsel. Don't isolate yourself in ethical ambiguity.
- *Act swiftly.* If risk is imminent, contact emergency services or a mental health crisis team. Do not delay.
- *Follow through.* Remain involved. Check in. Continue to offer spiritual support even if the person is hospitalized or transferred.

☐ *Field Tip:* Never say, "I won't tell anyone," unless you are absolutely certain the situation poses no risk. That promise can trap you—and cost lives.

Legal context: know your jurisdiction

Laws vary by state and country. Know what applies in your context. Some key differences:

- *Duty to warn vs. duty to protect*
    - *Warn* means notifying a third party (e.g., a potential victim).
    - *Protect* may mean hospitalization or intervention without notifying others.
- *Mandatory reporting*
    - Some jurisdictions require you to report self-harm threats; others allow discretion.
- *HIPAA and privacy*
    - Under HIPAA, you *may* disclose information if you believe it's necessary to prevent serious harm—and it aligns with state law.
- *Spiritual privilege*
    - In some states, clergy-penitent privilege protects confidential communi-

cation—even from legal disclosure. In others, it does not override the duty to protect.

☐ *Field Tip:* Ask your institution for a clear, written policy. Know the law—and your role within it.

The chaplain's role: sacred trust meets practical obligation

As spiritual caregivers, we are often the first to hear the unspeakable. We are not police. We are not judges. But we are *responsible*. When someone says, "I want to die," it's not just a confession. It's a moment of sacred vulnerability—and potential crisis.

How to respond:

1. *Stay calm.* Your presence is your power. Don't flinch.
2. *Clarify the situation.* Get details without interrogation.
3. *Affirm the person's humanity.* "Thank you for telling me. That was brave."
4. *Explain your obligation.* Gently. Clearly.

5. *Act decisively.* Safety over secrecy.
6. *Remain present.* Don't abandon the person once others are involved.

Chaplain Kara leaned forward. "Thank you for telling me. That's not easy. I hear that this pain feels overwhelming." Ethan nodded, swallowing hard. "I want you to know something," she continued. "What you're feeling matters. And your life matters. I'll do everything I can to walk through this with you—but I also have to make sure you stay safe. That means bringing in some help."

Ethan looked at her, a flicker of fear in his eyes. "Are you going to send me away?"

"I'm going to make sure you're not alone with this anymore," Kara said. "That's different."

Courage, clarity, compassion

Confidentiality is sacred. The duty to protect is sacred, too. One preserves *trust.* The other preserves *life*. Chaplains must carry both. *Confidentiality fosters healing. Duty to warn prevents tragedy. Together, they form ethical care.* Know your limits. Know your laws. But above all, know that your words, your presence, and your courage can change the story for someone who sees no way out. You might be the last person someone speaks to before they make a decision that can't be undone. Let that conversation be one that saves.

☐ *Reflection Points for Caregivers*

- When has someone shared something with you that felt dangerous to keep secret?
- How confident do you feel in balancing confidentiality with the duty to protect?
- Do you know your local laws and institutional policies on suicide risk and disclosure?
- How might fear—of being wrong, of breaking trust—keep you from acting?
- Who can you consult with when you feel uncertain about what action to take?

📋 *Action Checklist: Confidentiality and Duty to Warn*

✓ Explain confidentiality and its limits at the start of any spiritual care relationship.
✓ Stay calm and present when someone discloses suicidal thoughts.

- ✓ Ask directly about intent, plan, and access to means.
- ✓ Document all disclosures and actions taken.
- ✓ Consult with supervisors or legal advisors when in doubt.
- ✓ Act immediately if there is credible, imminent risk.
- ✓ Know your local laws and professional guidelines.
- ✓ Follow up with the individual after intervention—they still need you.

CHAPTER 6

The Silent Scream: Recognizing and Responding to the Warning Signs of Suicide

There are people who scream without making a sound. They smile while slipping away. They show up to dinner, lead worship, post funny videos, and then go home and stare at the ceiling until 3 a.m., wondering if anyone would notice if they stopped showing up. Sometimes they leave no notes. No final post. Just a gaping hole and a question that eats away at everyone left behind: *How didn't we see it?* That's the question we're going to face head-on in this chapter. You are here—reading this, training for this—because you never want to ask that question again. Let's learn how to listen to the screams the world has taught people to whisper.

What are the warning signs?

Suicide doesn't happen in a vacuum. It happens in the context of pain—often invisible, often denied—but rarely without clues. That's where *warning signs* come in. They are the subtle shifts, the phrases repeated too often, the disconnection behind the eyes of someone who says, "I'm fine." Understanding warning signs helps us catch someone on the edge *before* they fall. It moves us from reaction to prevention.

□ *Key Distinction:*

- ✓ *Risk factors* = long-term vulnerabilities (e.g., depression, trauma).
- ✓ *Warning signs* = immediate red flags that indicate an acute crisis.

Think of it like this: if risk factors are the general weather forecast—cloudy, chance of rain—then warning signs are the lightning and thunder, indicating an immediate storm.

The categories of concern

We group warning signs into three main categories: What They Say, What They Do, and How They Seem. Each one matters. Taken together, they tell a fuller story.

What They Say: Listening to the Echoes of Despair

"I can't do this anymore."
"You'll be better off without me."
"I don't want to be here."
"I wish I could disappear."

These aren't just emotional outbursts. They're *exit language*—veiled or direct clues that someone is thinking about leaving life behind.

Listen for:

- *Direct expressions of intent*
  "I'm going to kill myself."
  "I want to die."

These require immediate action. No exceptions.

- *Indirect statements*

"It'll all be over soon."
"I just want peace."

"You won't have to worry about me much longer."

- *Talk of hopelessness or being trapped*

"There's no way out."
"Nothing is going to change."
"I'm just a burden."

- *Saying goodbye or making amends*—Giving away prized possessions. Writing letters. Apologizing out of the blue.
- *Obsession with death or dying*—Frequent references to suicide, researching methods, or fascination with stories about death.

□ *Field Tip:* Don't dismiss indirect language. If it sounds like goodbye, *ask why.*

What They Do: Watching for Behavioral Shifts

Suicide isn't just spoken—it's acted out in subtle and not-so-subtle ways. Some people go quiet. Others go wild. What matters is *change*—especially sudden or unexplained changes in behavior.

Watch for:

- *Withdrawing from life*—No longer showing up for church, family events, or even text conversations.
- *Increased substance use*—Drinking more. Misuse of medication. Trying to *numb* the pain.
- *Risky behavior*—Driving recklessly, picking fights, taking unnecessary risks. As if they don't care what happens next.
- *Acquiring lethal means*—Buying a gun. Stockpiling pills. Googling *peaceful ways to die*. These are urgent warning signs.
- *Dramatic mood swings*—Especially a shift from deep despair to sudden calm or happiness. This can mean they've made a decision to die—and feel relief.
- *Changes in sleep and appetite*—Can't sleep. Sleeps all day. Stops eating. Eats constantly. These changes often mirror inner chaos.
- *Neglecting appearance*—Letting hygiene go. Appearing disheveled or disconnected from self-care.
- *Self-harm*—Cutting. Burning. Hitting oneself. These acts are not always suicide

attempts—but they indicate deep emotional pain and increased risk.

▢ *Field Tip*: If you notice two or more of these changes in someone, ask yourself: *What might this person be trying to express without words?*

How They Seem: Reading the Emotional Undercurrent

Some changes are harder to see—but they matter just as much. Suicidal ideation often reveals itself in someone's emotional state before it ever turns into action.

Feel for:

- *Depression*—Persistent sadness, flat affect, apathy, irritability, frequent crying.
- *Anxiety*—Restlessness. Tension. Panic attacks. Constant worrying.
- *Shame and humiliation*—Especially after personal failures, public embarrassment, or moral injury.
- *Loss of meaning*—Statements like, "None of this matters," or "I don't know why I'm still here."

- *Guilt or self-hate*— "I ruin everything." "Everyone would be better off without me."

□ *Field Tip*: You don't need a diagnosis to see emotional suffering. Trust your gut. If someone feels "off," check in.

Trusting your intuition

Let's talk about what chaplains often feel but struggle to name: That *uneasy sense* that something isn't right. Maybe they haven't said anything obvious. Maybe they're still showing up. But something inside you whispers: *Pay attention.* That's your intuition. It's not superstition. It's informed by thousands of micro-signals—body language, energy, tone—that your heart picks up before your mind can explain.

□ *Real Story*:

A youth pastor once called a student after hearing him sing one verse too quietly at worship. The kid broke down crying and admitted he'd written a suicide note that morning.

□ *Lesson*: Don't wait for certainty. Respond to the concern. Ask the question.

What you can say

Knowing the signs is one thing. Responding takes courage. Here's a guide to starting the hardest—and most important—conversation you may ever have. "I've noticed you've seemed different lately. I care about you. Can we talk about how you're doing?"

"Sometimes when people say things like 'I don't want to be here,' they're feeling really overwhelmed or even thinking about suicide. Is that where you are right now?"

"Are you thinking about hurting yourself?"

"Have you thought about how you would do it?"

"Do you have a plan or means to carry it out?"

Don't be afraid to use the word *suicide.* You won't plant the idea. You'll give them permission to tell the truth.

When they say yes

If someone says they're suicidal, here's what to do:

1. Stay calm. Panic helps no one. You are their anchor now.
2. Stay with them. Physically, emotionally, spiritually—until help arrives or you can get to it.
3. Remove means. If they have a weapon, pills, or another method nearby, do everything you can to remove access.
4. Don't promise secrecy. Say: "I can't keep this to myself because I care too much about you. We'll get through this together, but I need to involve someone who can help."
5. Call for help. Depending on the situation, this may mean:
    - 988 Suicide and Crisis Lifeline (USA)
    - A local crisis team
    - Emergency services
    - A mental health provider or on-call chaplain

Important considerations for chaplains and caregivers

You are not their therapist. Your role is to *listen*, *love*, and *link* to help. Don't carry the burden of diagnosis or long-term care planning. Be the bridge. Be the presence. But don't try to be everything.

You can't save everyone

And you shouldn't try. You are not the Messiah. But you can *be the moment*—the sacred interruption in someone's spiral toward death. And sometimes, that's all it takes.

You must care for yourself

This work will wear on your soul. Watching for warning signs in others can trigger exhaustion, hypervigilance, or compassion fatigue in you. Get support. Debrief with trusted colleagues. Make space for silence, prayer, and your own healing.

◻ *Remember:* You can't pour into others from an empty cup.

The conversation that saves

A few years ago, a seminary student named Leila confessed to her chaplain mentor that she had spent the last two nights deciding whether to end her life. She was functioning, leading worship, and submitting papers. No one knew, except her mentor, who noticed she had stopped singing, stopped joking, and started sitting in the back, closest to the exit. That mentor sat with her for two hours. No judgment. Just presence and steady questions. She didn't hospitalize her. She didn't fix her. But she named the storm and stayed through it. Leila is alive today because of that.

☐ *Reflection Points for Caregivers*

- Who in your life might be showing subtle warning signs? How might you check in?
- What phrases do you now recognize as potential cries for help?
- Have you ever been afraid to ask someone if they were thinking about suicide? Why?
- What helps you remain steady in the face of another's crisis?

- What support do *you* need to keep doing this work well?

📋 Quick Reference: Suicide Warning Signs

Talking:

- "I want to die."
- "I can't do this anymore."
- "Everyone would be better off without me."

Behavior:

- Withdrawing
- Risk-taking
- Giving things away
- Searching for lethal means

Mood:

- Hopelessness
- Anger or irritability
- Shame or guilt
- Sudden calm after turmoil

CHAPTER 7

When It Matters Most: How to Talk to Someone About Suicide

"I'm just so tired."

"It'd be easier if I weren't around."

"I just want it all to stop."

You hear these words. They land like smoke—thin, vague, easy to dismiss. But to the trained ear, they are something more. They are *invitations*. And if you're reading this chapter, then you are choosing to be someone who doesn't ignore the smoke. You are choosing to lean in, ask the hard questions, and walk with someone toward light when they're drowning in the dark. This chapter is your guide to that sacred conversation—the moment when everything hinges on how you listen, how you speak, and how you stay.

Angela had always been the quiet one in Bible study. Thoughtful. Kind. Always with a plate of cookies and a half-smile that never reached her eyes.

That night, she stayed after everyone left. Just stood there, mug in hand. "I shouldn't be here," she finally said.

The chaplain—Rev. Olivia—put down her own cup. She didn't ask what Angela meant. She asked, "Are you thinking about ending your life?"

Angela blinked, but she didn't look surprised. She looked relieved. "Yes," she whispered.

The power of the question

Let's begin here: *Asking someone if they're thinking about suicide does not increase the risk.* In fact, it might save their life. Most people struggling with suicidal thoughts *want* someone to notice. But they're terrified of what will happen if they tell the truth. They've rehearsed every version of rejection in their mind:

- "You're being dramatic."
- "You have nothing to be sad about."
- "You just need to pray more."

So instead of confessing outright, they offer clues—what we call *invitations*. Phrases like:

- "I just can't do this anymore."
- "Everyone would be better off without me."
- "I wish I could sleep and not wake up."

These aren't just expressions of pain. They are coded messages, asking, "Can I say the thing I'm really afraid of saying? Will you still love me if I do?"

How to begin the suicide conversation

Notice the signs

Before the conversation even starts, you have to *see* the person. That means paying attention to:

- Their language (see chapter 6).
- Their energy.
- Their withdrawal.
- Their eyes.

What you see

Say it gently. Clearly. With compassion. "I've noticed you've seemed really overwhelmed lately."

"You said something earlier that worried me—'I don't want to be here.' Can we talk about that?"

"You've been quiet. I'm wondering how you're really doing."

This is the *door-opener*. It tells them: *I'm not afraid of your pain. You're safe here.*

Ask the direct question

When it's time to ask, be direct. Say:

"Are you thinking about suicide?"

"Are you having thoughts of ending your life?"

"Have you thought about hurting yourself?"

It's okay to feel awkward. It's not about being perfect—it's about being *present*.

□ *Field Tip:* Don't say:

- "You're not thinking of doing something stupid, are you?"
- "You're not going to hurt yourself, right?"

These questions carry shame. They shut down honesty because they give the impression that the one asking desires a negative response.

When the answer is yes

This is the moment that freezes some people, but not you, because you're ready to do what matters most: *stay, listen, and love.*

Stay calm

Breathe. Slow your voice. Let them know you're not going anywhere.

"Thank you for telling me."

"I'm so sorry you've been carrying this alone."

"You don't have to go through this by yourself."

Don't try to fix it

This is not the moment for theology. It's not time to talk about *God's plan* or *counting blessings.* This is the time for presence. Let silence stretch. Reflect on what they say.

"That sounds incredibly painful."

"It makes sense that you're exhausted."

"You've been carrying so much."

Ask the four key questions

These will help you assess how immediate the risk is:

1. Are you thinking about suicide?
2. Do you have a plan?
3. Do you have access to the means, like a weapon or pills?
4. Have you ever tried before?

The more *yes* answers you get, the higher the risk.

If they're at immediate risk

If they say:

- Yes, they're thinking about suicide.
- Yes, they have a plan and means.

Then this is a *crisis*. It requires immediate action.

What to do:

- *Stay with them.* Don't leave them alone.
- *Remove the means* if it's safe (unload or hide firearms, take pills, etc.).
- *Call for help.* Dial *988* in the U.S. for the Suicide and Crisis Lifeline. If needed, call 911 and request a Crisis Intervention Team.

When calling 911, say: "This is a psychiatric emergency. The person is suicidal and at immediate risk. We need mental health response."

Stay calm. Stay near. Speak clearly.

If they're not at immediate risk

If they say:

- "Yes, but I don't have a plan."
- "I've thought about it, but I'm not going to act on it."

Then they're likely at *moderate risk.* Still serious and still needs support.

Here's what you do:

Affirm and thank them

"I'm so grateful you told me."
"You don't have to carry this alone anymore."
"You're not broken—you're human."

Help them connect to support

Offer to:

- Help them find a counselor.
- Sit with them while they call a helpline.
- Walk them through what support looks like.

Don't say, "You should see someone." Say, "Would it help if I helped you make that call?"

▢ *Field Tip:* Concrete help beats vague encouragement every time.

Create a safety plan together

If they're stable and open to it, walk them through a simple safety plan:

A good safety plan includes:

- *Warning signs*: "How will you know when you're slipping?"
- *Coping strategies*: "What helps you calm down?"
- *Support people*: "Who can you call at 2 a.m.?"
- *Professional help*: "Do you have a counselor or know where to find one?"
- *Safe environment*: "What needs to be locked away or given to someone else?"

Write it down. Keep it simple. Keep it real.

What not to do

Avoid:

- ✕ *Spiritual shortcuts:* "Just pray more." "Let go and let God."

- ✕ *Minimizing:* "You're overreacting." "It's not that bad."
- ✕ *Making it about you:* "Why didn't you tell me?" "You scared me so much."
- ✕ *Promises you can't keep:* "I won't tell anyone." (You might *have* to tell someone.)

Instead, promise this: "I'll walk with you through this. You don't have to do it alone."

After the conversation: what now?

Follow up

Send a message the next day.
Drop off coffee.
Ask, "How are you doing—*really*?"
This is the *lifeline*. Not the one conversation—but the consistent presence.

Get support for yourself

You can't carry the weight of someone's survival by yourself. Talk to a mentor, supervisor, or therapist. Debrief. Breathe. You were not built to do this alone.

Let go of outcomes

You can't control what someone chooses. You can only control how fully you show up. You are not responsible for their decisions. You are responsible for *being there*, fully human, fully present, and fully compassionate. And that can be enough. That can be everything.

☐ *Reflection Points for Caregivers*

- When has someone given you an *invitation*, and you didn't know how to respond?
- What makes you hesitant to ask someone if they're thinking about suicide?
- How can you become a better listener—not fixer—when someone opens up?
- Who will you debrief with when these conversations come to your door?

📋 *Suicide Conversation Checklist*

✓ Notice verbal or nonverbal *invitations*.
✓ Ask directly: "Are you thinking about suicide?"
✓ Stay calm and listen without judgment.

- ✓ Ask the four risk questions (thoughts, plan, means, history).
- ✓ Act immediately if the risk is high.
- ✓ Help connect to mental health support.
- ✓ Create a safety plan if possible.
- ✓ Follow up within twenty-four to forty-eight hours.
- ✓ Take care of yourself after the conversation.

CHAPTER 8

Instructions for Filling Out the Stanley Brown Safety Plan for Suicide Prevention

The Stanley Brown Safety Plan for suicide prevention is a critical, personalized document. It empowers individuals by outlining concrete steps they can take when experiencing suicidal thoughts or urges. The goal is to provide immediate, actionable strategies to manage distress and connect with support, keeping the individual safe until the intensity of the crisis diminishes.

Important considerations before you begin:

- ✓ *Be honest and specific:* The more accurate and detailed you are, the more effective the plan will be.

- ✓ *Collaborate:* Ideally, complete this plan with a trusted mental health professional (chaplain, therapist, counselor, psychiatrist). They can offer guidance and ensure the plan is comprehensive.
- ✓ *Keep it accessible:* Once completed, keep the plan in a place where it's easily accessible but also secure. Share it with trusted individuals if you feel comfortable.
- ✓ *It's a living document:* Your plan isn't static. Review it regularly (e.g., monthly, or after significant life changes) and revise it as needed.

Sections of the Stanley Brown Safety Plan (and how to fill them out):

I. **Warning signs (internal and situational triggers)**
   - **Purpose:** To identify the very first signs that you are starting to experience suicidal thoughts or urges. These are your personal *red flags.*
   - **How to fill out:**
     - **Internal warning signs:** What are the thoughts, feelings, physical sensations,

or internal experiences that tell you a crisis is approaching?

♣ *Examples:* "Feeling hopeless," "isolating myself," "intense anxiety," "sleeplessness," "replaying negative thoughts," "a specific bodily sensation (e.g., tightness in chest)."

- **Situational triggers:** Are there specific situations, places, or events that tend to bring on these warning signs or increase your suicidal thoughts?
  - ♣ *Examples:* "Being alone at night," "anniversaries of losses," "arguments with loved ones," "financial stress," "hearing certain news."
- **Action:** List three to five specific warning signs. Be as precise as possible.

II. **Internal coping strategies**

- **Purpose:** These are things you can do *on your own*, without involving anyone else, to distract yourself or soothe yourself when you notice warning signs.
- **How to fill out:**
  - Think about activities or techniques that genuinely help you feel calmer,

more grounded, or distracted from distress.

- *Examples:* "Listening to specific calming music," "going for a walk," "reading a book," "watching a favorite movie/show," "deep breathing exercises," "practicing mindfulness," "taking a warm bath," "engaging in a hobby (e.g., drawing, knitting, playing an instrument)," "writing in a journal."
- **Action:** List three to five activities or strategies. Be specific about what you will do.

III. **Social supports (non-professional distraction/support)**

- **Purpose:** These are people you can contact who can provide a distraction or offer support, but *who are not necessarily professionals* or involved directly in your mental health care.
- **How to fill out:**
  - Identify people whom you trust, who are good listeners, and who make you feel safe or cared for.
  - *Examples:* "A close friend," "a family member (e.g., sibling, parent,

aunt/uncle)," "a mentor," "a spiritual advisor."

- **Action:** List at least two to three people, their names, and their phone numbers. Briefly note *what kind of support* they might offer (e.g., "distraction by talking about work," "just listening," "watching a movie together").

IV. **Professional help and resources**

- **Purpose:** These are mental health professionals or crisis services you can contact for direct support when you are in a crisis.
- **How to fill out:**
  - **Current mental health providers:**
    - ♣ List your therapist/counselor's name and phone number.
    - ♣ List your psychiatrist/doctor's name and phone number.
  - **Crisis hotlines/services:**
    - ♣ National Suicide and Crisis Lifeline: Dial **988** (in the US) or other national crisis lines relevant to your country.
    - ♣ Local Crisis Line: If there's a specific local crisis line you know.

    - ♣ Crisis Text Line: Text "HOME" to 741741.
  - **Emergency services:**
    - ♣ Emergency Services (Police/ Ambulance): **911** (in the US) or your local emergency number.
    - ♣ Nearest Emergency Room/ Hospital: Provide the name and address.
  - **Action:** List all relevant professional contacts and emergency resources with their numbers/addresses.

V. **Making the environment safe (reducing access to lethal means)**

- **Purpose:** To make it harder to act on suicidal urges by limiting access to means that could be used to harm oneself. This is a crucial step.
- **How to fill out:**
  - **Identify means:** Think about any items or methods you might consider using if you were to act on suicidal thoughts (e.g., medications, firearms, sharp objects, ropes, specific locations).

- Plan for restriction: How will you make these less accessible during a crisis?
    - *Examples:* "Giving all prescription medications to a trusted friend for safekeeping," "having a family member secure firearms and ammunition elsewhere," "removing sharp objects from my immediate environment," "avoiding specific high-risk locations."
- **Action:** List specific items and the concrete steps you will take to reduce your access to them. This section is often best completed with the help of someone you trust.

VI. **Reasons for living/reasons for hope**

- **Purpose:** To remind yourself of what matters to you, what you value, and what you have to live for, even when distress is overwhelming.
- **How to fill out:**
    - Think about people, pets, future goals, experiences, values, or beliefs that give your life meaning and purpose.

  - *Examples:* "My children/family," "my pet," "finishing my degree," "traveling to X," "experiencing Y," "helping others," "my faith," "the simple joy of a sunrise."
  - **Action:** List three to five specific reasons. You might even include a photo or small memento alongside this section when you use the plan.

Review and commitment:

- **Review:** Before finalizing, read through the entire plan. Does it feel realistic? Is it specific enough? Are there any gaps?
- **Commitment:** The plan usually includes a space for your signature and date, signifying your commitment to using it when needed. If a professional helped you, there might be a space for their signature too.

CHAPTER 9

After the Storm: Walking with the Bereaved Through Suicide Loss

When the phone rings at 2:14 a.m., it never rings with good news. Pastor Ben Thomas sat upright in bed, still half-asleep, as the words reached him over the line: "It's Marcus. He died tonight. Suicide." There it was. The unspoken fear is now spoken. Ben whispered a prayer under his breath. Then he got dressed and headed to the family's home, not to offer answers—he had none—but to offer presence. That's what postvention begins with: *presence*, not prescriptions.

What is postvention?

Postvention is the compassionate, practical, and sustained support of those affected by suicide. It is:

- ✓ Holding a grieving mother who can't speak.
- ✓ Sitting in silence with a teenager whose best friend just died.
- ✓ Organizing a safe memorial for a school without romanticizing death.
- ✓ Helping a community name the pain and begin to heal.

Postvention is not crisis management alone. It's not a single visit. It's a *process*—of grief, support, listening, reweaving shattered meaning.

Why postvention matters

Suicide loss is different. It shatters. It isolates. It silences. Those left behind face a particular storm of grief:

- ✓ *Stigma* that makes others uncomfortable to even say the word.

- ✓ *Guilt* that loops on repeat: *"What did I miss?"*
- ✓ *Blame*—of self, others, the system, even the deceased.
- ✓ *Abandonment*, because it feels like a choice, even when it wasn't.
- ✓ *Relief*, in rare cases, for loved ones exhausted from caregiving—a relief almost always soaked in shame.

And when this kind of pain isn't addressed, it grows. Grief becomes trauma. Silence becomes suffering. In some cases, *contagion* follows—especially among youth or in close-knit communities.

☐ *Reality Check:* Survivors of suicide loss are at significantly higher risk of experiencing suicidal ideation themselves.

That's why this chapter matters.

The nature of suicide grief

There's no roadmap. No neat timeline but understanding the terrain can help you walk with others who've been thrust into it.

Common emotional experiences:

- *Shock and disbelief*—even if the death seemed *predictable.*
- *Anger*—toward the deceased, toward God, toward themselves.
- *Confusion*—the relentless and unanswerable *why.*
- *Shame*—fueled by social discomfort and spiritual misunderstanding.
- *Guilt*—often illogical, but always intense.
- *Loneliness*—people withdraw because they don't know what to say.

For families, dynamics shift:

- Parents may grieve differently from siblings.
- Children may regress, act out, or internalize blame.
- Spouses may wrestle with anger and abandonment.

For peers and coworkers:

- The death feels both close and strange.
- They may fear being judged for *not noticing.*

And for *you*, the caregiver, there's your own grief—plus the burden of carrying theirs.

Principles of postvention care

These are your guiding stars. Keep them close.

Compassion and empathy

Show up. Be human. Hold space for rage, sobbing, silence.

No answers required. Just presence.

"I'm here. I don't have the right words. But I'm not going anywhere."

Non-judgment and de-stigmatization

Say "died by suicide," not "committed suicide."

Avoid theology that assigns shame.

Educate gently. Normalize grief.

"You're not alone. This kind of grief is complicated—and valid."

Safety and risk assessment

In early conversations, gently assess:

- Are others in the household also at risk?
- Are there suicidal thoughts present?
- Do they have access to means?

If yes, connect to *immediate* crisis support. Remove means if safe.

Practical support

Don't say, "Let me know if you need anything."
Say:
"Can I bring dinner on Thursday?"
"Do you want help making the calls?"
"I can sit with the kids during the funeral."
Concrete offers > vague sympathy.

Information and education

People crave understanding. Provide resources about:

- The grief process.

- Support groups.
- Counseling.
- Books or pamphlets about suicide bereavement.

Cultural sensitivity and autonomy

Respect how the person's culture and beliefs shape their grief. Let them lead. Don't push for catharsis. Let them grieve in their way.

Long-term support

Grief doesn't end at the funeral. Check in after a month. After three. On the anniversary. Healing happens in *repetition*, not rescue.

Timeline of support

A. Immediate Response (first twenty-four to seventy-two hours)
   For individuals:
   - Be present. Don't fill the silence.
   - Provide water, warmth, grounding.
   - Offer tissues *without interrupting*.

- Ask: *"What do you need right now?"* Not: *"How are you feeling?"*

For communities (schools, churches, workplaces):

- Activate a *crisis team.*
- Designate *point people* for communication.
- Control misinformation. Clarify what is known.
- Create *safe spaces* for processing and prayer.
- Avoid public speculation or glorified tributes.

B. Short-Term Support (Week 1 to month 3)

- Help survivors connect with grief counselors.
- Recommend local or online support groups.
- Continue practical help—childcare, meals, errands.
- Normalize symptoms of traumatic grief (sleeplessness, rage, numbness).

☐ *Field Tip:* Ask: "Would you like me to check in again in a few days?"—and then do it.

C. Long-Term Support (three months and beyond)
  - Anniversaries are hard. So are holidays. Mark them.
  - Encourage rituals that honor the person *without defining them by their death.*
  - Support survivors becoming advocates if it helps them heal.

Suicide contagion and prevention

Yes, suicide can influence others—especially those who are vulnerable. But this is *not* about blaming the deceased or shaming grief. It's about being *proactive*:

- Don't share graphic details.
- Avoid romanticizing or framing the death as an *escape*.
- Frame suicide as a tragedy of unrelieved pain—not a solution.
- Create safe dialogue: "If you're struggling like they were, help is available."

Protective factors:

- Open conversations about mental health.
- Clear pathways to counseling.

- Compassionate leadership.
- Grief rituals that honor life, not method.

How to communicate

Say this:
"I'm so sorry for your loss."
"I don't have the right words, but I'm here with you."
"Would you like to talk about them?"
"This isn't your fault."
"Whatever you're feeling is okay."
Avoid this:
✕ "Why did they do it?"
✕ "At least they're at peace now."
✕ "Everything happens for a reason."
✕ "You'll move on eventually."
□ *Field Tip:* You can't fix this. You can *witness* it. That's what heals.

Caring for yourself as a postvention provider

This work can hollow you out if you're not careful. Signs of *secondary trauma*:

- Emotional exhaustion.

- Numbness or overidentifying.
- Avoidance of certain topics.
- Hypervigilance or nightmares.

Self-care is not optional.

- Debrief regularly. With someone safe and skilled.
- Maintain personal therapy if needed.
- Practice boundaries. You are not the sole savior.
- Rest. Sleep. Walk. Pray. Journal.
- Remember: *Their grief is not yours to carry alone.*

National resources

- **988 Suicide and Crisis Lifeline**—Call or text 988 anytime.
- **Crisis Text Line**—Text HOME to 741741.
- **AFSP (American Foundation for Suicide Prevention)**—afsp.org
- **SPRC (Suicide Prevention Resource Center)**—sprc.org
- **The Dougy Center (for grieving children and families)**—dougy.org

The chair at the end of the pew

Six months after Marcus died, his mother—Denise—came back to church for the first time. She sat at the end of the pew, near the exit. Reverend Ben walked over quietly. No fanfare. Just sat beside her. She didn't cry. She didn't speak. But she reached for his hand. That was the moment postvention became *presence again.* Not about fixing. Not about finding answers. Just one hand in another, surviving grief together.

Most people will not remember what you say, but they will always remember that you were there.

☐ *Reflection Points for Caregivers*

- Have you ever felt unsure how to support someone after a suicide loss? What held you back?
- What internal beliefs about suicide might shape how you show up?
- How do you respond to your own emotional pain after supporting someone else's?
- What boundaries or rhythms help you avoid compassion fatigue?

Postvention Support Checklist

- ✓ Show up within twenty-four to seventy-two hours if possible
- ✓ Use compassionate, non-stigmatizing language
- ✓ Offer concrete help: food, childcare, planning
- ✓ Normalize grief reactions and trauma responses
- ✓ Encourage counseling and support groups
- ✓ Watch for signs of suicide risk in others
- ✓ Educate the community to prevent contagion
- ✓ Follow up regularly—especially on anniversaries
- ✓ Debrief and care for yourself consistently

CHAPTER 10

Rebuilding After Loss: Restoring Life, Meaning, and Hope

Grief doesn't ask for your permission. It doesn't knock. It breaks the door open and rearranges your life. After a suicide, grief becomes a landscape you didn't choose to live in—but must learn to walk through. The questions echo:

Why?

What could I have done?

How do I go on without them?

And the deeper, quieter one:

Do I even want to?

This chapter is about that next chapter. Not closure. Not forgetting. But *rebuilding*—with trembling hands and stubborn hope.

The garden no one tended

Every Saturday morning for three months, Maria sat in the chair beside her son's empty bedroom. She didn't speak. She didn't cry anymore. She just sat—still, hollowed. Then one morning, she walked into the backyard. She picked up a trowel. And without knowing why, she began to clear weeds from the flower bed her son used to help her tend. That's what rebuilding looks like. Not a grand epiphany. Just one small act of defiance against despair.

What does healing look like after a suicide loss?

It looks like contradiction:

- Laughing one moment, breaking down the next.
- Finding meaning in a memory and anger in the same breath.
- Waking up one day without the weight—and then feeling guilty for it.

Healing is not linear. It's not neat. It's spiral-shaped. It loops and revisits, regresses, and rises.

▢ *Field Tip:* Tell the grieving person:

"Whatever you're feeling today is valid. There's no right timeline."

The work of rebuilding

Grieving fully

Healing starts with *allowing grief*—not avoiding it. That includes:

- *Naming the loss.* Avoid euphemisms. Say the truth: *"He died by suicide."*
- *Telling the story.* Let the person talk—over and over, if needed.
- *Holding complexity.* It's okay to feel love, anger, guilt, and gratitude all at once.

"I miss her—and I'm mad at her."

"I feel relieved he's not in pain—and crushed he's gone."

Grief holds all of it.

Reconnecting with the body

Trauma lives in the body. After a suicide loss, people often disconnect:

- They stop eating.
- They can't sleep.
- They feel numb or hypersensitive.

Help them come back gently:

- Encourage walking, yoga, grounding exercises.
- Suggest creative outlets like art, music, gardening.
- Guide them toward sleep hygiene and hydration.

The body is not separate from the soul. It is the instrument of healing.

Finding a safe community

Isolation is a toxin in suicide grief. Survivors need spaces where:

- They can talk without explaining.
- They are not judged.
- They are not pitied.

Encourage:

- Suicide loss support groups.
- Peer gatherings through AFSP or local organizations.
- Church communities are willing to engage with trauma truthfully.

If no such space exists, help create one.

■ *Real Story:* After her daughter's death, a mother launched a monthly grief circle in her church basement. Two years later, twenty-three people gather regularly to share their stories.

Reclaiming meaning

This is the most sacred and difficult part: *Rebuilding life's meaning after it's been shattered.* This doesn't mean justifying the death. It doesn't mean saying, "Everything happens for a reason." It means:

- Discovering how to live with *and* beyond the pain.
- Asking: *What do I still love? What do I want to create? Who do I want to become in the wake of this?*

Some survivors write. Some advocate. Some raise awareness. Some just keep showing up—and that's enough. Help them find:

- A purpose beyond the pain.
- A reason to keep going, even if it changes week to week.

Building rituals of remembrance

Healthy remembrance integrates the lost person into ongoing life, without making their death the defining story. Support survivors in:

- Creating a memory table or scrapbook.
- Holding a candle lighting on birthdays.
- Sponsoring a bench, tree, or scholarship in their name.
- Telling stories about the *life* they lived, not just the way they died.

☐ *Field Tip:* Invite this reflection:
"What's something about them you'd want the world to remember?"

For survivors who struggle to rebuild

Sometimes, survivors get stuck in complicated grief. Signs include:

- Persistent, debilitating guilt or shame.
- Avoiding reminders of the person entirely.
- Inability to engage in daily life months after the loss.

- Intense anger or withdrawal that does not soften over time.

In these cases, professional therapy—especially trauma-informed grief counseling—is vital. Offer to help find support. Say:

"You don't have to carry this alone. Would it be okay if I helped you find someone to talk to?"

For chaplains and caregivers: how you can help

Your role is not to rescue. It is to *remain.*

Here's what rebuilding support looks like:

- *Long-term checking in.* Not just at the funeral. At six months. At a year. On holidays.
- *Spiritual accompaniment.* Helping people wrestle with God, purpose, hope, prayer—even doubt.
- *Creating honest spaces.* Where grief and faith can coexist without one silencing the other.
- *Affirming worth.* Guilt corrodes identity. Keep reminding them: *"You did the best you could with what you knew."*

- *Inviting new dreams.* Gently ask: *"Is there anything you want to do this year just for yourself?"*

■ *Field Tip:* Recovery isn't about moving on. It's about moving forward with what cannot be changed—and choosing to live anyway.

What hope looks like after a suicide loss

Hope is not glitter or sunshine. Hope is:

- A garden that gets weeded again.
- A laugh that feels unburdened, even for a second.
- A survivor showing up to help someone else.
- A prayer spoken in the dark.

Hope says: "This grief is real, but it doesn't get the final word."

The scar and the seed

Two years after her brother died, Janelle stood at the front of the sanctuary and lit a candle. "I didn't think I'd ever speak in public again," she said. "I didn't think I'd find peace. But I realized that grief doesn't disappear—it gets planted." She looked at the room full of other survivors. "And from it, something can grow. I'm here because I chose not to burn down the garden."

□ *Reflection Points for Caregivers*

- How do you define hope for yourself in the context of deep loss?
- What internal pressures or expectations do you carry about how others *should* grieve?
- Have you witnessed someone begin to rebuild? What did that look like?
- What gives you the strength to keep showing up for others, even in the face of unfixable pain?

Rebuilding Support Checklist

✓ Encourage full and honest grief.
✓ Help survivors reconnect with their body through rest, activity, and nourishment.
✓ Suggest safe, stigma-free support communities.

- ✓ Affirm the right to grieve without judgment or timeline.
- ✓ Support rituals of healthy remembrance.
- ✓ Invite small acts of hope or purpose.
- ✓ Watch for signs of complicated grief and refer appropriately.
- ✓ Offer presence, not pressure.
- ✓ Check in long after others have stopped.
- ✓ Care for your own soul as you care for theirs.

CHAPTER 11

Staying Human: Building Sustainable Ministries of Suicide Prevention

You've heard the hardest words. You've held hands in emergency rooms. You've wept in pews, prayed by graves, sat beside people unraveling. And still, you're here. Still listening. Still learning. Still *showing up*. This chapter is for you—for the ones who chose presence over comfort, compassion over certainty. And now, the question becomes:

How do we keep doing this work—well, wisely, and without losing ourselves?

Suicide prevention is a ministry

Make no mistake: this is sacred work. To talk to someone from the edge is to kneel at the threshold of life and death. To accompany someone through loss is to stand on holy ground. But if we're not careful, we reduce this work to responses—crisis calls, funerals, referrals. Prevention becomes *reactive* instead of *relational.* Sustainable suicide prevention is not just about managing emergencies. It's about *building a culture of care*—where it's safe to struggle, where no one is invisible, and where hope has a place to live.

Laying the foundation: a culture of safety

A suicide-safe community doesn't happen by accident. It must be built. Here's how.

Normalize mental health conversations

Preach about it. Pray about it. Put it in bulletins. Talk about therapy like you talk about physical checkups.

☐ *Field Tip:* Use the pulpit to say:

"Mental illness is not a weakness. Depression is not a sin. Asking for help is an act of courage."

Train your people

Offer regular workshops on:

- ✓ Suicide awareness
- ✓ Listening skills
- ✓ Mental health first aid
- ✓ Crisis response

Equip small group leaders, teachers, ushers—everyone. You don't have to train clinicians. You just have to train *humans* to notice, care, and refer.

Establish clear protocols

What happens when someone says, "I want to die"? Too many communities freeze. Or worse, they panic and overreact. You need a plan:

- Who is the point of contact?
- What outside professionals are on call?
- What's your step-by-step flow?

■ *Reality:* Systems save lives. Compassion without structure can lead to chaos.

Build partnerships

You're not alone. Connect with:

- Local crisis lines and clinics
- School counselors
- Peer support organizations
- Faith-based therapists
- Suicide prevention coalitions

If you can't find a partnership, form one.

Ministering without burning out

This is tender work. And if we're honest, it takes a toll. So let's talk about *you.*

Know your limits

You are not a therapist (unless you are). You are not a savior. You are not invincible. You are a presence. A guide. A voice of care. Your role is sacred, but it is also *finite.*

Build a support system for yourself

- Schedule regular debriefs with colleagues.
- Meet with a supervisor or spiritual director.
- Make room for your own emotions—your grief, anger, weariness.
- Journal. Exercise. Get enough sleep. Laugh. Breathe.

Practice Sabbath

Silence is not a luxury. Rest is not laziness. Even Jesus walked away from the crowds. Block out time—weekly or monthly—to unplug from caregiving. Let your soul be restored, not just your schedule reset.

☐ *Field Tip:* Ask yourself weekly: "What do I need to be well enough to keep showing up?"

Name the toll—and the meaning

Suicide prevention will break your heart. It will also save your life. It will show you the depths of human resilience. It will remind you why compassion still matters in a divided world. Hold the ache but also hold the beauty.

■ "I've seen someone choose life who was certain they wouldn't. That moment stays with me," said a hospital chaplain.

Legacy: what you leave behind

When people remember your ministry, they won't remember your sermons or your credentials. They'll remember:

- That you asked the hard question with gentleness.
- That you didn't flinch when they said, "I don't want to live."
- That you didn't disappear after the funeral.
- That you listened without fixing. Held without judging. Stayed without rushing.

That's the legacy of a suicide prevention ministry. Not programs. Not numbers. But presence.

The life that stayed

Two years ago, James almost didn't make it. He had the plan. The means. The moment was picked out. Then his church's youth leader—just a guy with a guitar and a big heart—noticed something. He said something. "Hey, you okay? You've been quiet lately. Want to talk?"

That was the beginning. One conversation. One question. One lifeline. Today, James leads a support group for others. He says it every time:

"It wasn't a sermon that saved me. It was a person who stayed."

☐ *Final Reflection*

- What have you learned about your own capacity for presence and compassion?
- Where do you still feel afraid or uncertain—and what support do you need?
- What would it mean to create a truly suicide-safe community in your care setting?
- Who will you train, equip, or mentor in this work?
- What kind of legacy do you want to leave behind?

📋 *Final Commitments Checklist*

- ✅ I will speak openly and compassionately about suicide.

- ☑ I will listen without judgment and ask directly when concerned.
- ☑ I will know when to connect someone to professional help.
- ☑ I will support those grieving with presence, not platitudes.
- ☑ I will build structures and teams for prevention and postvention.
- ☑ I will take care of myself as I care for others.
- ☑ I will never underestimate the power of showing up.

FINAL BLESSING

May your hands be steady when others tremble.
May your heart stay open, even when it breaks.
May your voice speak courage to silence.
May your presence be a place of safety.
And may you always remember:
You are not alone. You are never alone.
You carry light. Let it stay lit.
Amen.

APPENDIX A

Suicide Risk Assessment Questions

Use these questions as conversation tools—not interrogations. Tone, empathy, and timing are essential. Adapt language for age, culture, and context.

Exploring Suicidal Ideation (SI)

Passive SI:

- "Do you ever feel like life isn't worth living?"
- "Have you ever wished you could just go to sleep and not wake up?"
- "Do you think people would be better off without you?"

Active SI:

- "Have you thought about ending your life?"
- "Have you imagined how you might do it?"

Assessing Suicidal Intent

- "Do you want to die?"
- "Are you thinking about taking your own life?"
- "Do you intend to go through with it?"

Follow-ups for ambivalence:

- "Do you want the pain to end, or do you want your life to end?"
- "What's keeping you here right now?"

Evaluating Plans and Means

- "Have you thought about how or when you would do it?"
- "Do you have access to the things you'd need to carry out your plan?"
- "Have you done anything to prepare, like writing a note or giving things away?"

Exploring Protective Factors

- "Is there anything or anyone that's stopping you?"

- "Have you had thoughts like this before and gotten through them? What helped?"
- "Who would you want to talk to right now?"

⚖ Gauge Impulsivity and Recent Triggers

- "Have things changed suddenly in your life?"
- "Have you acted on impulse before when you were feeling overwhelmed?"

APPENDIX B

Risk-Tier Response Chart

This chart helps caregivers determine the appropriate level of intervention based on a person's expressed suicidal ideation, intent, and plan. Always consult mental health professionals when possible.

Risk Level	Indicators	Response
Low Risk	Passive SI only. No intent or plan. Expresses some hope. Has protective factors.	– Offer emotional support – Create a safety plan – Provide referrals – Schedule follow-up
Moderate Risk	Active SI without a clear plan or intent. Some ambivalence. May lack protective factors or show signs of distress or withdrawal.	– Escalate supervision – Develop a written safety plan – Refer to a mental health professional

High Risk	Active SI with a plan and/or access to means. Strong intent. History of attempts or high impulsivity.	– Do *not* leave a person alone – Remove means – Contact the crisis team or emergency services
Imminent Risk	Expressed intent to act *now*, or recent attempt. Has a plan, means, and no protective factors.	– Call 911 or equivalent – Initiate emergency hospitalization – Stay with the individual

☐ **Note for chaplains and caregivers:**

When in doubt, escalate. You are not responsible for fixing or diagnosing, but you are responsible for responding. Your presence, clarity, and compassion can be the bridge to lifesaving care.

APPENDIX C

Stanley-Brown Safety Plan

STANLEY - BROWN SAFETY PLAN

STEP 1: WARNING SIGNS:

1. ______
2. ______
3. ______

STEP 2: INTERNAL COPING STRATEGIES – THINGS I CAN DO TO TAKE MY MIND OFF MY PROBLEMS WITHOUT CONTACTING ANOTHER PERSON:

1. ______
2. ______
3. ______

STEP 3: PEOPLE AND SOCIAL SETTINGS THAT PROVIDE DISTRACTION:

1. Name: ______ Contact: ______

2. Name: ______ Contact: ______

3. Place: ______ 4. Place: ______

STEP 4: PEOPLE WHOM I CAN ASK FOR HELP DURING A CRISIS:

1. Name: ______ Contact: ______

2. Name: ______ Contact: ______

3. Name: ______ Contact: ______

STEP 5: PROFESSIONALS OR AGENCIES I CAN CONTACT DURING A CRISIS:

1. Clinician/Agency Name: ______ Phone: ______
Emergency Contact : ______

2. Clinician/Agency Name: ______ Phone: ______
Emergency Contact : ______

3. Local Emergency Department: ______
Emergency Department Address: ______
Emergency Department Phone : ______

4. Suicide Prevention Lifeline Phone: 1-800-273-TALK (8255)

STEP 6: MAKING THE ENVIRONMENT SAFER (PLAN FOR LETHAL MEANS SAFETY):

1. ______
2. ______

Stanley-Brown
Safety Planning Intervention

APPENDIX D. EPIDEMIOLOGY

Suicide by the Numbers

Globally, nearly eight hundred thousand people die by suicide each year, according to the World Health Organization. For every suicide death, there are an estimated 20–25 attempts. Suicide is the fourth leading cause of death among individuals aged 15–29, and 77 percent of suicides occur in low- and middle-income countries, highlighting deep disparities in mental health access and support.

In the United States, the numbers are equally sobering:

- *2022:* 49,476 suicide deaths.
- *2023 (preliminary):* Slight decline, but still over 49,000.

Suicide ranks:

- *The second leading cause of death* for ages ten to fourteen and twenty-five to thirty-four.
- *The fourth leading cause* for adults aged thirty-five to forty-four.
- Demographic Variations
- *Age*: Suicide rates are highest among middle-aged and older White males, often overlooked in public discourse focused on youth.
- *Gender*: Men die by suicide nearly four times more often than women, largely due to method lethality (e.g., firearms). Women attempt more frequently but with less lethal means.
- *Race/Ethnicity*:
    - *American Indian/Alaska Native*: Highest rate (26.8 per 100,000).
    - *White*: 17.7 per 100,000.
    - *Black*: Rising rates, especially among youth (9.4 per 100,000).
    - *Hispanic or Latino*: 7.5 per 100,000.
    - *Asian/Pacific Islander*: 6.8 per 100,000.

These statistics must be contextualized. Demographic groups are not monolithic. Factors like age, gender identity, geography, and cultural background intersect and affect risk.

High-Risk Populations

- *LGBTQ+ individuals* face elevated risk due to discrimination, rejection, and a lack of affirming spaces.
- *Veterans and military personnel* often experience PTSD, moral injury, and reintegration stress.
- *First responders and healthcare workers* face chronic trauma, burnout, and organizational barriers to mental health care.
- *Rural populations* often struggle with isolation, stigma, and limited access to services.

Understanding the Data

Sources:

- *Vital statistics*: Death certificates compiled by the CDC.
- *Medical examiner reports*: Offer contextual details.

- *Hospital discharge data*: Captures medically treated attempts.
- *Surveys*: Track ideation and non-lethal behaviors (e.g., Youth Risk Behavior Survey).

Limitations:

- *Underreporting*: Suicides may be misclassified due to stigma or uncertainty.
- *Data lag*: Most national data is one to two years behind.
- *Non-fatal attempts*: Often go unrecorded if medical care is not sought.
- *International inconsistencies*: Differences in how countries define and report suicide.

ABOUT THE AUTHOR

David Carr is a chaplain, certified mental health coach, and suicide prevention advocate with over a decade of experience in pastoral care. With a bachelor's degree in Pastoral Ministries and Bible from Columbia International University, David has spent years supporting individuals and families in crisis, providing guidance, comfort, and intervention. As a QPR-certified trainer in suicide prevention, he has helped countless people navigate the delicate and critical moments of life-threatening distress. He has a heart for helping others find hope in their most difficult times, which is the driving force behind his book, *The Suicide Conversation*.

www.ingramcontent.com/pod-product-compliance
Lightning Source LLC
LaVergne TN
LVHW090415210926
848480LV00002B/572
9798896179856